Moshi Monsters™
monsters

D1635163

Music Stars

H46 603 249 1

Published by Ladybird Books Ltd 2013
A Penguin Company
Penguin Books Ltd, 80 Strand, London, WC2R 0RL, UK
Penguin Books Australia Ltd, 707 Collins Street, Melbourne, Victoria 3008, Australia
Penguin Group (NZ), 67 Apollo Drive, Rosedale, Auckland
0632, New Zealand (a division of Pearson New Zealand Ltd)
Sunbird is a trademark of Ladybird Books Ltd

Written by Jonathan Green

www.ladybird.com
001
Printed in Slovakia

ALWAYS LEARNING   **PEARSON**

Helloooo, Moshi music fans! The name's Ruby Scribblez, editor of Shrillboard Magazine, and I'm here to give you the lowdown on all the Moshi music stars!

Ruby: I'm joined by the greatest talent scout in Monstro City – the ultimate pop-tastic music mogul, Simon Growl himself. Hi, Simon! It's such an honour to interview you!

Simon: Hi Ruby. And yes it is, isn't it?

Ruby: So, Simon, what can fans expect when they check out the Moshi music scene?

Simon: Well, there are some familiar faces right alongside some unexpected rising talent and even a couple of brand new gooperstars in the making.

Ruby: Tell me more!

Simon: Well, first up there's Bobbi SingSong, one of the most talented Moshlings to sign to HighPants Productions, who comes all the way from Jollywood. And then there's the sassy singer, Missy Kix, who's already big in far-off Moshimo City.

Ruby: Simon, that sounds goopendous!

Simon: Oh it is, Ruby. It is. Rather like me.

We'll be hearing more from Simon later, along with other guest writers including gossip queen Tyra Fangs, Bubba the Bouncer from the Underground Disco, and HighPants Productions' latest signing - the mysterious Missy Kix herself! But what else can you look forward to in this exclusive exposé? Well, there's everything from tips on how to make it in the Moshi music biz and a sneaky peak behind the doors of the most amazing Moshi cribs, to an interview with the totally goo-licious Zack Binspin and a glimpse of what it's like backstage at a Music Rox gig. So what are you waiting for? It's time to totally Rox out!

Contents

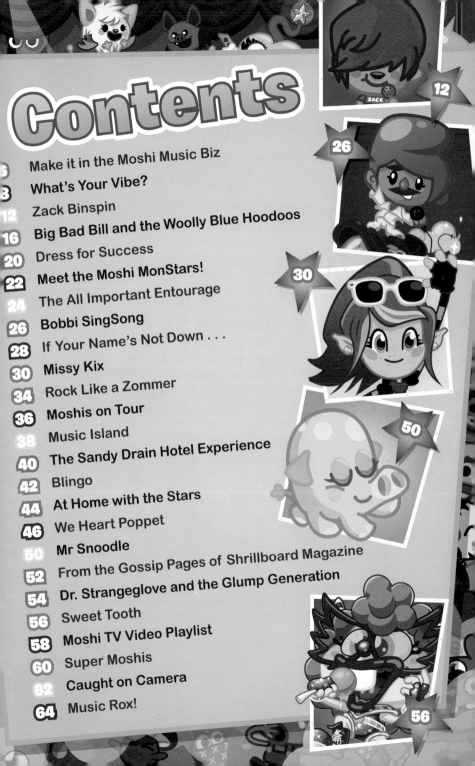

Make it in the Moshi Music Biz

Hi! I'm Simon Growl, President, Owner and Founder of HighPants Productions, Talent Scout, Producer and H.A.R.G.G. – that's Handsome All Round Good Guy, in case you were wondering. I mean, how could it be anything else?

What I don't know about the music business isn't worth knowing. I've got the coolest look, the greatest hair and a totally fabulous singing voice. Sort of. But look, I can't spend all day talking about myself. Well, actually, I could, but Ruby's asked me to give you the goss on how you can make it in the music biz and become almost as famous as me in the process. Of course, not everyone can be as handsome or as talented as I am, so for all you lesser mortals here are my top five tips for making it big.

1 Make sure you look completely goopendous. If you don't look like a star no one's ever going to believe you are a star. I mean, look at that goofy, hair-obsessed Moptop.

No, not Zack Binspin. He's totally unbelievably roarsome. The other one. You know who I mean, with his ridiculous high-pitched warbling.

2 Once you've got your look, find yourself a mega-famous manager ... like the head of HighPants Productions, perhaps.

3 With a fangtastic manager there also comes a hits factory that will write the perfect song to launch you on to the Moshi music scene.

4 Everyone's talking about recycling these days and there's no better way to get a Top Ten hit than by raiding the back catalogue of some has-been act and recycling their greatest hits for a new generation.

5 Failing that, just slip a few music execs a bucket load of Rox and before you know it, you could have a top ten hit all of your own!

THE Underground DISCO

Judge, Jury and Top Producer

As well as being a Moshi music mogul and founder of HighPants Productions, Simon Growl is also a celebrity judge at Monstro City's Underground Disco, along with Roary Scrawl and Tyra Fangs – although it's Simon who **always seems to give the lowest scores.**

What's Your Vibe?

What genre of music is the one that's guaranteed to get you putting on your dancing shoes? If you hope to become the next Missy Kix or Bobbi SingSong, what would be the kind of music you'd like to play?

Check out these musical styles to give yourself some ideas . . .

Clearly Classical

Some people might think this style of music is as dead as the composers who first made it popular yonks ago – Moshis like Goatzart, Furi Feethoven and Raaahms – but **Twirly Tiddlycopters just love to play classical music** when they're swooping over Monstro City!

Hoodoo

It's the **hip jungle vibe** that throbs through the Gombala Gombala Jungle. If limbo's your thing then you'll soon be **swaying like crazy** to its up-tempo beats. Big Bad Bill and the Woolly Blue Hoodoos love to limbo to this funky rhythm, as is clear from their breakthrough hit 'Go Do the Hoodoo'.

Drool Metal

Characterised by heavy guitars, loud drums and deep growling vocals, it's the heavy rock sound that's been made popular all over again by rising Roxstar, Zommer. You don't need to be able to **remove your own arm and use it as a drumstick**, of course, but what can I say . . . It helps!

MUSIC

Jollywood Jive

Like a faster version of Singaling Swing, Jollywood Jive is an **energetic musical and dance style** popular in the lands east of Music Island. The Jollywood Jive is fast and energetic, full of fierce pumping beats – accompanied by pointy hand gestures and dancing sideways across the stage. It's becoming increasingly popular in Monstro City, thanks to the **mantra-inspired warblings** of Jollywood legend Bobbi SingSong.

Moshimo City Pop

Electronic dance music that's hit the big time in far-off Moshimo City, it has its origins in rock but is now purely pop. Features lots of melon twistatrons, squiddledex, digiplops and other sound effects. Missy Kix's breakthrough track 'The Missy Kix Dance' is Moshimo City pop at its finest!

Gooey Glam Rock

Gooey Glam Rock is a style of rock and pop music performed by singers and musicians who wear outrageous clothes, make-up and hairstyles, particularly platform boots and plenty of glitter. With its catchy chorus lines and thumping beats, once it's in your head it's hard to get it out again!

Skidoo-bap-diddly-pap Ska

Skidoo-bap-diddly-pap Ska combines bits of Hoodoo Calypso and Jeepers Creepers Jazz, not to mention Roarberry rhythm and blues. The lyrics are really just a lot of old skiddly-doo-bap nonsense.

ck Binspin, the Moptop weenybop, is the hottest tar to come out of Simon Growl's stable of gooperstars in a looooong time (and is way cooler than that other Moptop Tweenybop you might have heard of – and has MUCH better hair). I'm pleased to say he's also a close personal friend of yours truly, Ruby Scribblez.

Ruby: Hi Zack, it's great to see you again.

Zack: You too, babe.

Ruby: Your hair's looking great by the way.

Zack: I know.

Ruby: I have to ask – because I know there are some Moshis out there who have already asked themselves the same question – what do you say to those people who claim you're just copying . . . well . . . you know who's look?

Zack: I would say to those critics, have you heard that other Moptop sing? I mean, he can't! Why would I want to copy someone who can't sing? No, I'm the real deal, babe.

Loyal fans: You love you, Zack!

Ruby: So . . . Anyway . . . Your single, 'Moptop Tweenybop', was a massive hit.

Zack: Thanks to all my loyal fans!

Loyal fans: You love you, Zack!

Zack: I know.

Ruby: As well as your goopendous, heart-breaking, pitch-perfect vocals, the track features Blingo, the Flashy Fox. How did that collaboration come about?

Zack: He's my homie. He's like me – slick, cool and super funky.

Ruby: Now I'm sure what your loyal fans are dying to know is –

Loyal fans: We love you, Binspin!

Zack: I know.

Ruby: – where does the coolest Moptop Tweenybop in town hang out?

Zack: Brashcan Alley, with my crew of course. Or with my manager, Simon Growl, at the Sandy Drain Hotel on Music Island.

Ruby: How cool is that?

Zack: Hey, Ruby, why don't you drop by my dustbin later and we can snuggle in the grime.

Ruby: Sounds totally amaaazing! I'll see you later. Save me a mutant sprout!

LIVING THE DREAM

Zack Binspin has dreamt of being a famous singer ever since he saw Screech McPiehole yelling on Top of the Mops – and now he's even bigger than Screech himself!

13

MOPTOP TWEENYBOP

(MY HAIR'S TOO LONG)

Hey . . . you wanna stroke my hair? It's okay . . . it's just me,
Zack, Zack Binspin
Hey, check out my lid. It's real rusty
Conditioner? No, this is just goo baby

I live in a funky dustbin
Surrounded by trash
We're talking 'bout mutant sprouts
And lumpy, gone-off mash

Yeah, I gotta funny hairdo
But hey, that's okay
If you run your fingers through it, it's like a buffet

Moptop Tweenybop
Shimmyin' an shakin'
I've lost count of the hearts that I've been breakin'
I can't see and my eyeballs they are achin', cos my
hair's too long

I hang out in Brashcan Alley
With my band and my crew
If you were a true believer, you'd be there too

Yeah, I know that I'm a heart throb
But that ain't a crime
So check out my dustbin, baby
We can snuggle in the grime

Moptop Tweenybop
Shimmyin' and shakin'

I've lost count of the hearts that I've been breakin'
I can't see and my eyeballs they are achin', cos my
hair's too long

I'm here with my homies in the crazy world of Moshi
Rappin' for my buddy even though he's wishy washy
Slamming down the rhymes like a rusty dustbin lid
Blingo the Fox?! Duetting with a kid?
Moptop Tweenybop shimmyin' and shakin'
Sittin' on his groove, you know that I ain't fakin'
Holy guacamole, I just gotta rap more slowly
Cos I'm runnin' outta breath and
these tempos kinda throw me

Moptop Tweenybop
Shimmyin' an shakin'
I've lost count of the hearts that I've been breakin'
I can't see and my eyeballs they are achin', cos my
hair's too long

We love you, Binspin
I know!

UDIGWOTSGOINDOWN?

Slick, cool and super funky, Blingo the
Flashy Fox never takes off his shades
because all that gleaming bling he wears
is totally dazzling!

BIG BAD BILL
AND THE
WOOLLY BLUE HOODOOS

...se and mystical, naturally ...omadic and strangely scared of ...easpoons, wandering Woolly Blue ...oodoos travel great distances ...n their search for enlightenment, bald peaches and deep fried Oobla Doobla. Big Bad Bill's travels have taken him from the sweltering Gombala Gombala Jungle to the Moshi Monsters' first album Music Rox!

I managed to secure a **rare interview** with the Woolly Blue Hoodoo himself, and his manager, Simon Growl - although I have to admit, **it didn't quite go as I had imagined . . .**

Ruby: So Bill . . . Can I call you Bill?

Bill: Oobla Doobla gombala.

Ruby: Er, okay.

Simon: He says, yes, Bill is fine.

Ruby: So, Bill, what do you think of the current music scene?

Bill: Gombala gombala wallawalla hoohaa!

Simon: I think what Big Bad Bill's trying to say is that he thinks it's a heap of old Oobla Doobla.

Ruby: Oobla Doobla?

Bill: Oobla Doobla?

Wallawalla hoohaa Oobla Doobla!

Ruby: I'm sorry? Oobla Doobla?

Simon: It's his favourite.

Ruby: Yeah, I kinda got that.

Bill: Oobla Doobla!

Simon: Fried and served in coconut shells. Oh, and he's quite partial to purple bananas too.

Ruby: Purple bananas?

Bill: Gombala wallawalla hoohaa!

Simon: And moonlit gazelles, of course.

Ruby: But of course.

Simon: So, when does my star get to perform his track?

Bill: Gombala gombala wallawalla hoohaa! Oobla Doobla wallawalla hoohaa! Mba-wanga-thlunk!

GO DO THE HOODOO

Big Bad Bill is a Woolly Blue Hoodoo

Deep in the jungle friends kept disappearing
Sent out a search party they found a clearing
There stood a Moshling all woolly and blue
Stirring a cauldron of hot hoodoo stew
Singin' . . .

Lotions and potions and hexes and spells
Strange creepy crawlies and sweet jungle smells
Fried Oobla Doobla in coconut shells
Purple bananas and moonlit gazelles

Don't look now but I think I heard a twig crack!
Don't look now but I think I heard a twig crack!
Don't look now but I think I heard a twig crack!
Don't look now but I think I heard a twig crack!

Wiping his fur due to great jungle heat
Bill started pounding a fierce tom tom beat
Putting the limbo bar lower and lower
Accompanied by rumblings from Mount Krakka Blowa

Big Bad Bill he's a-gonna throw a party
Big Bad Bill he's a-gonna throw a party
Big Bad Bill he's a-gonna throw a party
Big Bad Bill he's a-gonna throw a party

Lotions and potions and hexes and spells
Strange creepy crawlies and sweet jungle smells
Fried Oobla Doobla in coconut shells
Purple bananas and moonlit gazelles

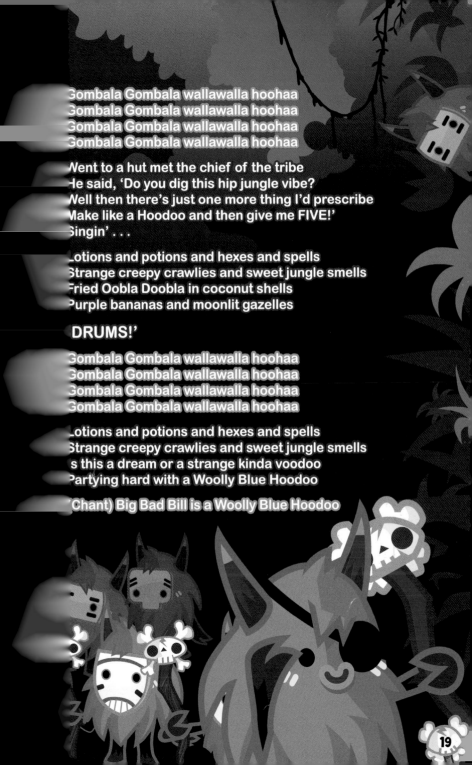

Gombala Gombala wallawalla hoohaa
Gombala Gombala wallawalla hoohaa
Gombala Gombala wallawalla hoohaa
Gombala Gombala wallawalla hoohaa

Went to a hut met the chief of the tribe
He said, 'Do you dig this hip jungle vibe?
Well then there's just one more thing I'd prescribe
Make like a Hoodoo and then give me FIVE!'
Singin' . . .

Lotions and potions and hexes and spells
Strange creepy crawlies and sweet jungle smells
Fried Oobla Doobla in coconut shells
Purple bananas and moonlit gazelles

'DRUMS!'

Gombala Gombala wallawalla hoohaa
Gombala Gombala wallawalla hoohaa
Gombala Gombala wallawalla hoohaa
Gombala Gombala wallawalla hoohaa

Lotions and potions and hexes and spells
Strange creepy crawlies and sweet jungle smells
Is this a dream or a strange kinda voodoo
Partying hard with a Woolly Blue Hoodoo

(Chant) Big Bad Bill is a Woolly Blue Hoodoo

Dress for Success

Hi fashion fans and all you wannabe trend-setters! Ruby's invited me to talk to you about how to dress for success on the Moshi music scene and give you a few pointers about looking good.

If you're going to be a chart-busting Rox music gooperstar, it's not enough that your song's good and you sound good - you have to look good too.

To make it in the world of Moshi music you need to find the look that works for you and then work it. And of course, if you need any advice, you can always check out my tips in *The Daily Growl*.

What's Hot And What's Not!

BLING

Okay, so bell-bottoms, polyester and platforms are out, but if rap's your thing, then bling is in. Just check out Slingo, that flashiest of Flashy Foxes. Curly moustaches look sooo good too! And don't forget your shades. Blinging!

MOSHIMO MIX

If Missy Kix is more your style, why not try re-creating the Moshimo City look for yourself? You'll need to track down cool trainers and fingerless gloves, then layer up with stripy tops and tights, and maybe even a rah-rah skirt. Don't forget the sunglasses again – only this time wear them on top of your head!

GOOGEOUS

If looking cool and making your fans swoon is your thing, then get yourself a Moptop Tweenybop hairstyle like Zack Binspin's. Remember, you'll need plenty of goo if you're going to pull off that look yourself – and plenty of hair!

ROCK

Zommer's full of drool and way too cool for school. Stitch yourself into some ripped threads and mix 'em up to capture his totally grungy look.

Meet...
THE MOSHI MONSTAR

Ruby: Hey, Moshi music fans, I'm here with the real stars of the music scene – the Moshi MonStars! Hi guys!

MonStars: Hi Ruby!

Ruby: So, tell me about your sudden and unexpected rise to fame.

Furi: Well, Ruby, all six of us auditioned at Growl Mansion in front of Simon himself, Tyra Fangs and Simon's Wiggy Thingy. It was part of High Pants Productions' Monstro City's Got The Ex-Idol Pop Factor competition.

Ruby: I bet that was nerve-wracking!

Poppet: Yes it was, but we just went for it and did our best.

Ruby: Nobody could ask you to do more.

Luvli: But then, when we finished Simon said, "I don't see a single recording artist," ... Well, we each thought our dreams of becoming the Next Big Thing had just gone up in smoke.

Furi: But then he went on saying, "I see six recording artists. Guys, from now on you're the Moshi MonStars!" We were over the moon!

Diavlo: I almost exploded I was so excited!

Zommer: I jumped up and down so much one of my arms fell off.

Ruby: So, what's the plan now?

Zommer: Oh, it's okay. I stitched it back on.

Katsuma: Now? We plan to kick the likes of Sweet Tooth and Strangeglove off the charts!

Ruby: Good luck with that! And thanks for taking the time to talk to me.

Moshi MonStars: Bye, Ruby!

THE MOSHI MONSTERS THEME

"Ladies and gentlemen, boys and girls, introducing the most goopendous monsters in the swooniverse!"

Moshi Monsters, number one
Moshi Monsters, crazy fun
Moshi Monsters, gloop and goo
Moshi Monsters, Moshi Monsters

Have you ever seen a critter with a crater for a head?
Or a heap of hair that looks as if it just got outta bed?
Or a rocker sewn together with some slimy bits
of threada?
Moshi Monsters laa laa laa

Have you ever been enchanted by a floaty woaty thing?
Or partied with a furry friend who boogies
when you sing?
Or watched a ninja kitty kung fu fightin' balls of string?
Moshi Monsters laa laa laa

Woah-oh! Yeah. Hands in the air!
Woah-oh! Yeah. Okay!

[Chorus]
Moshi Monsters, number one
Moshi Monsters, crazy fun
Moshi Monsters, gloop and goo
Moshi, Monsters, Moshi Monsters
Moshi Monsters, fangs and claws
Moshi Monsters, soft cute paws
Moshi Monsters, squeals and yelps
Moshi Monsters, Moshi Monsters

Well think of all the monsters that you've ever sung about
Most of them are scary all they do is growl and shout
But Moshis are the monsters we just couldn't be without
Moshi Monsters laa laa laa

So meet the monsters in Monstro City
Where the grass is green and they sing this ditty
You can sing-along and swing-along, and wiggle till
you're giddy
Moshi Monsters laa laa laa

Woah-oh! Yeah. Hands in the air!
Woah-oh! Yeah. Okay!

"Ladies and gentlemen, boys and girls, Monsters and
Moshlings . . . raise your hands in the air, now shake your
hair. Then wiggle your feet to the Moshi beat . . ."

[Repeat chorus]

The All Important
Entourage

Plinky
the Squeezy Tinklehuff

These squeezy-wheezy musical **Moshlings** like nothing more than having their keys tickled as they boing up and down, **puffing out merry tunes** and waltzing around town. But don't push their buttons – it makes 'em **hiccup out of tune!**

Wallop
the Jolly Tubthumper

Bashing yourself in the face with a pair of drumsticks isn't crazy – it's **totally bonkers!** B where else are these tip-tappin Moshlings supposed to practis their paradiddles? Besides, Jo Tubthumpers love drumming, and their **thwacktastic bodies are brilliantly boingy.** Drum roll please!

True gooperstars are always followed around everywhere they go by their own all important entourage, a group of friends and helpers who always have their star's best interests at heart. The most harmonious of Moshlings, the Tunies, make the perfect crew. These lil' rockers love to make sweet music, so for a budding Missy Kix or Zack Binspin what could be better?

Oompah
the Brassy BlowyThing

Do you like parping? Good, 'cause these melodious Moshlings can't stop tooting thigh-slapping tunes whenever they smell sausages grilling or hear wobble-ade fizzing. Brassy BlowyThings also enjoy burping rainbow-coloured bubbles as they march along to their toot-tastic ditties. Parp!

HipHop
the Blaring Boombox

Blaring Boomboxes are the playful noisemakers who just can't stop rockin' to the bang beat boogie that blares from their speakers day and night. Obsessed with old-school tunes, they love sharing their music with other Moshlings. Just make sure you don't press their 'record' button because it erases their memories. Oops!

Bobbi SingSong

Bobbi SingSong is already a gooperstar in his native Jollywood (turn left out of the Sandy Drain Hotel on Music Island, over the keyboard bridge, and keep heading east) and since signing to Simon Growl's HighPants Productions, this Singaling Moshling's name is now known throughout the whole Moshiverse.

Ruby: Hi Bobbi. In your breakthrough hit, 'Welcome to Jollywood', you say that you're a Moshling with a mantra. But what is your mantra?

Bobbi: I . . . um . . . I can't remember. But it doesn't matter. Ask me something else.

Ruby: O-kay . . . What kinds of wheelz does the hippest, jolliest Moshling in Jollywood use to get from A to B?

Bobbi: Why, my super-cool motorized rickshaw, of course. I think Blingo's expression is 'Blinged to the max'.

Ruby: So, how do you like to kick back after some serious sitar playing and making your Jollywood moves on stage?

Bobbi: After a tour I retreat to my very own yoga retreat.

Ruby: Yogurt retreat? Yum! What's your fave flavour?

Bobbi: Oh no, yoga, not yogurt! It's less fruity, more bendy. The retreat is where I meditate and focus on my mantra.

Ruby: Oh yes, your mantra . . . What was that again?

Bobbi: I . . . I've forgotten.

JOLLY GOOD IN JOLLYWOOD

The Jollywood Singaling's smash hit 'Welcome to Jollywood' is so popular in his homeland that it's been adopted as Jollywood's national anthem!

Welcome to Jollywood

(Welcome to) Jollywood Jollywood jolly good
Jollywood Jollywood
Jollywood Jollywood jolly good Jollywood Jollywood
Jollywood Jollywood jolly good Jollywood Jollywood
Jollywood Jollywood jolly good Jollywood Jollywood

Welcome don't you dilly dally
This might send you quite doolally
Introducing a sensation
Subject of great adulation

Flown from a mystical land east of here
Hot spicy flavours and hip atmosphere
With lots of colours and fierce pumping beats
Where Moshi rickshaws cruise bustling streets

I can make you move like Bobbi Bobbi SingSong
(He can make you groove like Bobbi Bobbi SingSong)
I can make you move like Bobbi Bobbi SingSong
(He can make you groove like Bobbi Bobbi SingSong)

Head to the left then head to the right
Arms akimbo legs real tight
Fingers up and twitch your neck
Judder sideways hit the deck
One step here and one step there
Shake those hips and brush your h h h h h . . .

[Chorus]
Jollywood Jollywood jolly good Jollywood Jollywood
Jollywood Jollywood jolly good Jollywood Jollywood
Jollywood Jollywood jolly good Jollywood Jollywood
Jollywood Jollywood jolly good Jollywood Jollywood

See steamy jungles, explore mountains high
Watch mystic gurus, sit back kiss the sky
Go wiggle jingling bells on your wrist
Pretzel yourself in a yoga-style twist

I can make you move like Bobbi Bobbi SingSong
(He can make you groove like Bobbi Bobbi SingSong)
I can make you move like Bobbi Bobbi SingSong
(He can make you groove like Bobbi Bobbi SingSong)

Head to the left then head to the right
Arms akimbo legs real tight
Fingers up and twitch your neck
Judder sideways hit the deck
One step here and one step there
Shake those hips and brush your h h h h h . . .
(It is jolly good in Jollywood!)

Taking tea on my verandah
Goodness me things things could not
be grander
I'm a Moshling with a mantra
Errrr, I've forgotten what it is . . .
it doesn't matter!

[Repeat chorus]

27

IF YOUR NAME'S NOT DOWN... ○ ○ ○

It's my job to make sure only the hippest Moshis and Moshlings get into a happening place like the Underground Disco - night spot of choice for the likes of Simon Growl and Tyra Fangs.

So, if you want to make sure you're granted an Access All Areas pass to all the coolest hang-outs in Monstro City and beyond, you could do a lot worse than check out my top five tips for making sure you don't miss out.

DID YOU KNOW?

THE TOP FIVE HIP HANG-OUTS

The Underground Disco
The Sandy Drain Hotel
The Hard Sock Café
Blingo's Blinged-Up Crib
Growl Mansion

TOP FIVE TIPS FOR GETTING INTO GIGS

1. Have a number one single and be the monster to be seen with.
2. Say your brother's cousin's friend's neighbour is Tyra Fang's hairdresser.
3. Pull your trousers up really high, put a Tubby Huggishi on your bonce and pretend to be Simon Growl.
4. Buy the bouncer a bottle of Wobble-ade. Or five.
5. If that fails, slip them a pawful of Rox.

He Ain't Heavy, He's My Brother

Bubba's brother has recently been appointed **Zack Binspin's bodyguard**. It's easy to tell Bubba and his bro apart because Bubba has a scar over his right eye, but his brother's is on the left!

As well as working as a nightclub bouncer, Bubba is a **well-known tattoo artist**. When's he not hanging out down at the Underground Disco, he likes to practise his flashy moves on his Dance, Dance, Roarvolution machine.

Missy Kix is the sassy singer all the way from far-off Moshimo City. She's already a mega-gooperstar over there and has taken the rest of Moshi World by storm.

Ruby: Hi Missy – welcome to Monstro City. What can you tell us about your single, 'The Missy Kix Dance'?

Missy: Whaddya wanna know? It's the coolest dance track that's getting everyone bouncing. It's pure Moshimo City pop with a Missy Kix twist.

Ruby: It is hyper-catchy. It really makes me wanna boogie.

Missy: Awesome, thanks!

Ruby: How are you finding it spending so much time away from your home in Moshimo City?

Missy: It's cool. I love Monstro City, especially the shops. I've been doing A LOT of shopping.

Ruby: Apart from shopping, what do you like to get up to in your spare time?

Missy: Er . . . Spare time? What's that?

Ruby: So the rumours of your moonlighting missions are unfounded?

Missy: Well, when I'm not in the goodio, or on stage, doing interviews or meeting my super cool fans, I've got . . . er . . . a lot of other things going on, which really doesn't leave a lot of time for anything else.

Ruby: Oh, OK. I'm sure whatever you're up to is fabulous!

Missy: Yeah, it is. But hey, I've gotta dash! You know, things to do . . . See ya!

The Missy Kix Dance

Are you ready for the show?
Shake your body to and fro
Clap your hands and feel the flow
Then spin around
Don't get flustered by the beat
Let the music guide your feet
Reconfigure then delete
Let's hit the street

Every Moshi's talkin' about the latest thing
But I just wanna boogie, party and sing
Every Moshi's talkin' about the latest thing
And guess what's in?

Leader of the fashion pack
I'm pumping up the glam
But other acts just wanna throw their toys out of the pram
Can you keep a secret I'm a Moshi on a mission
I'm Missy Kix, the sassy secret agent musician

Every Moshi's talkin' about the latest thing
But I just wanna boogie, party and sing
Every Moshi's talkin' about the latest thing
And guess what's in? The Missy Kix Dance!

Aa-ah aah, you gotta jump on in
Aa-ah aah, the Missy Kix Dance!
Aa-ah aah, you gotta jump and spin
So jump right in, the Missy Kix dance!

I'm a chic but deadly beauty
I'm a star that's set to stun
You can call me when you need me, I can be your number one
When danger comes a knockin' you'll know just who to ring
I'm Missy Kix the undercover Moshi who can sing

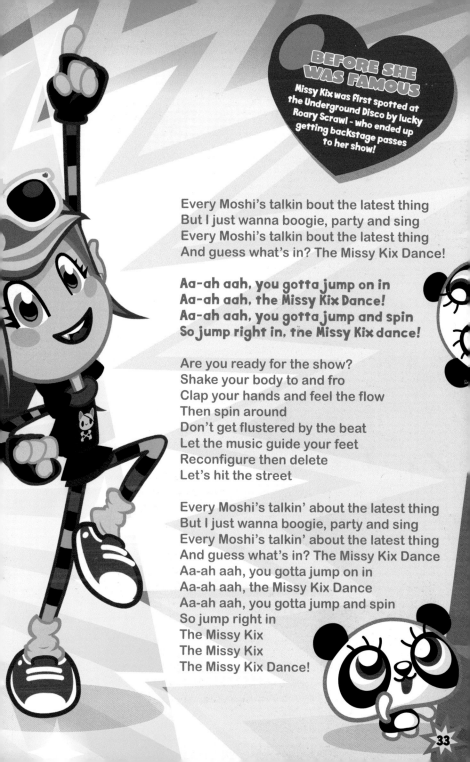

Every Moshi's talkin bout the latest thing
But I just wanna boogie, party and sing
Every Moshi's talkin bout the latest thing
And guess what's in? The Missy Kix Dance!

Aa-ah aah, you gotta jump on in
Aa-ah aah, the Missy Kix Dance!
Aa-ah aah, you gotta jump and spin
So jump right in, the Missy Kix dance!

Are you ready for the show?
Shake your body to and fro
Clap your hands and feel the flow
Then spin around
Don't get flustered by the beat
Let the music guide your feet
Reconfigure then delete
Let's hit the street

Every Moshi's talkin' about the latest thing
But I just wanna boogie, party and sing
Every Moshi's talkin' about the latest thing
And guess what's in? The Missy Kix Dance
Aa-ah aah, you gotta jump on in
Aa-ah aah, the Missy Kix Dance
Aa-ah aah, you gotta jump and spin
So jump right in
The Missy Kix
The Missy Kix
The Missy Kix Dance!

ROCK LIKE A ZOMMER

If Drool Metal's not really your scene - and it's certainly not mine - you might want to stick some barfmallows in your ears for this next bit . . .

Ruby: It's a combination of different musical influences – and that's just the recycled rock sensation Zommer!

Zommer: Totally rad dudette!

Ruby: So, Zommer, you're the champion of the Drool Metal rock sound, but what do you say to those critics who claim that Drool Metal has had its day and is, in fact, dead?

Zommer: What are you talking about? Drool Metal totally Rox the scene, you dig?

Ruby: Well it certainly smells like something around here's been dug up . . .

Zommer: Hey, I'm like all the Ro 'n' roll greats stitched into one.

Ruby: What do you say to those Moshis who say that your music

ROCK LIKE A ZOMMER

You've got fists . . . USE 'EM!
You've got fists . . . USE 'EM!

Stitch! Drool! Seams! Zommer! HEY
Stitch! Drool! Seams! Zommer! HEY

Livin' in the fast lane that's just the way I'm made
Got an appetite for goo and a thirst for wobble-ade
You got me rockin' like a Moshi got me rollin' like
a Glump
Banging my head you know you make me
wanna jump

I feel like I'm in pieces and my seams are fit to burst
My eyeballs they're a-popping and the itchin's
even worse
Turnin' up the volume this is Zommer metal heaven
Gonna party in the moshpit gonna crank it to eleven

Blowin' up the speakers till the walls begin to shake
The neighbours ain't complaining cos they dig the
noise I make
Jumbled up and drooling as I rock along the street
You know that I ain't fooling and I never miss a . . .
beat

Zommerific widdling!
Yo, Grandad! If it's too loud
you're too old!

Well do you wanna?
Do what you wanna?
Rock like a Zommer?
And bang your head?

Wait a minute!
Let's do it one
more time . . .

s too loud?

Zommer: I say, "Yo,
Grandad! If it's too loud
you're too old! We're
taking this one up
to eleven!"

Ruby: Well, thanks for
taking the time to talk
to us, Zommer.

Zommer: No worries,
man. Let's rock!

THIS IS A REMIX
Did you know that
Zommer produced
a remix of Zack Binspin's
single, 'Moptop Tweenybop
(My Hair's Too Long)?'
It totally rocked!
(Of course.)

35

MOSHIS ON TOUR

So when the Moshi MonStars and HighPants Productions' other acts go on tour, which venues do they play? How do they travel between gigs? And what do they simply have to have backstage so that they can kick back and relax when they're not on stage?

TOP FIVE VENUES

The Moshi MonStars – The Roaring Smallbert Hall
Zommer – The Wobble-ade Stadium
Bobbi SingSong – The Jollywood Bowl
Sweet Tooth – Hard Sock Café
Zack Binspin – Sandy Drain Hotel

TOP FIVE MODES OF TRANSPORTATION

Simon Growl - Private jet
The Moshi MonStars - The Moshi MonStars tour bus
Bobbi SingSong - Motorized rickshaw
Dr. Strangeglove - The Baddielac 9000
Sweet Tooth - Candy Cruiser

ROARSOME REQUESTS!

Music stars are notorious for the strange demands they make before agreeing to perform at a gig. Some of these conditions have gone down in Moshi Music history. I've managed to get hold of the star's requests from the latest Music Rox tour . . .

1 **The Moshi MonStars** – foam guitars so they can practise smashing up their instruments in safety.

2 **Big Bad Bill** – fried Oobla Doobla in coconut shells, purple bananas and half a dozen moonlit gazelles.

3 **Zack Binspin** – a fishbone comb and goo for hairstyling, and a gaggle of adoring fans to scream 'We love you, Binspin,' at the stage door.

4 **Zommer** – twenty-six bottles of wobble-ade, all the goo he can eat, his Stratoblaster guitar and an amp that goes all the way up to 12!

5 **Bobbi SingSong** – hot spicy snacks, jingling bells, his sitar, tea and his mantra (if anyone can remember what it is).

6 **Missy Kix** – pumps, Dance, Dance, Roarvolution machine and Yummy Gummies with all the purple ones taken out.

7 **Dr. Strangeglove and the Glump Generation** – Cloncomatic wrench, his gold-tipped cane, Scrummy Cupcakes, and a tin of trombone polish.

8 **Sweet Tooth** – enough sugary drinks and candies to send a dentist running for the door! And no savoury snacks!

9 **Poppet** – a pink dressing room, pink Yummy Gummies, pink Moshi Cupcakes, a photo album of her favourite Moshlings, a fresh vase of pink rox flowers . . . Whatever she wants, everything has to be pink!

10 **Super Moshis** – Slurp Slurp Slushies and Chocolate Coated Broccoli for energy, extra tights in case they get a ladder in them, and a Roarby cape press.

MUSIC ISLAND

SIMON GROWL'S PRIVATE AIRSTRIP

Welcome, Moshi music fans, to Music Island – or, as I like to call it, 'Where The Magic Happens'.

Anybody who's anybody hangs out here, and no monster can consider themselves a proper gooperstar until they're chilling out by the pool at the Sandy Drain Hotel with me and my celebrity friends.

But you wouldn't like it here on Music Island . . . you would absolutely love it! Hanging out at the Sandy Drain Hotel, drinking Essence of Blue with the likes of Zack Binspin and Blingo – how utterly fangtastic would that be?

Of course, if you ever get bored hanging out by the pool drinking wobble-ade, you could always go for an adventurous trek in the Gombala Gombala Jungle, snacking on fried Oobla Doobla in coconut shells with Big Bad Bill and the other Woolly Blue Hoodoos, or take a trip over to Jollywood, where I discovered the Singaling legend, Bobbi SingSong, and chill out with the musicians who play there all day.

38

GOMBALA GOMBALA JUNGLE

KEYBOARD BRIDGE

JOLLYWOOD

TV STUDIOS

MOSHI TV STUDIOS

SANDY DRAIN HOTEL

High Pants Productions

My good friend Tyra Fangs helped me choose who should go on the Moshi Monsters Music Rox album. She doesn't know anything about music, but she looks totally goopendous, so at least she knows what a gooperstar looks like. Besides, my best friend Binitta was away on holiday at the time.

We spent ages making our final decision. We even asked my wiggy thingy for a bit of advice, but it was too busy humming all the toe-tapping songs I've written to comment.

MUSIC ISLAND

The Sandy Drain Hotel Experience

Cascade — cool off under the crashing waterfall.

Guitar-shaped pool — chill out beside it or even take a dip in it. Just don't get that moptop wet.

Beach — go for a stroll along the hotel's private beach and chill your paws in the surf.

Gourmet restaurant — rammed to the rafters with only the most delectable delicacies.

So where do our Moshi megastars like to hang-out when they're not on tour? Plenty of them have their own cool cribs to chillax in – and we'll be checking out some of them later – but there's one place that every gooperstar likes to check out – or rather, check into – sooner or later for a bit of R&R . . . and that's the Sandy Drain Hotel. Here's why . . .

Gombala Gombala Jungle – the adventurous can go in search of the Lost Temple. (Don't blame us if you get lost and end up in a cauldron of hot hoodoo stew.)

Spa huts – keep that facial fur looking fresh with gooey monster-makeover treatments.

Extremely Exclusive

The Sandy Drain Hotel is a **highly exclusive hang-out**, for celebrities only – unless you happen to have a spare 5 million Rox to hand. That's how much it costs to stay at the Sandy Drain – **per night!**

BLINGO

Blingo the Flashy Fox is the funky fly rapper every rising gooperstar wants to work with. Known for his rap-tastic lyrics - that he delivers in his strange, lightning-fast language - he's the super slick DJ and MC all the Moshi musicians want to lay down some radical rhymes over their latest pop track.

DIGGIN YA LINGO

B.L.I.N.G.O. I rock the mic you rock the disco
(Tell me Bling baby what you wanna do
You're oh so fly and I'm digging you)

I said H.E.L.L.O. I'm a flashy little Fox by the name of Blingo
Slick, cool, super funky, my goatee's trim and my bling's
real chunky
Looking pretty fly 'cos I'm hitting the town
Cruising up to Main Street checkin' out what's going down
It's a colourful place where you can have good times
And that's diggity wiggity cool 'cos this verse all rhymes

Blingo Blingo digging your lingo
Top down, seat back, paw out the window
Blingo Blingo tongue in a twist
Rocking the mic, cranking out hits
(Repeat)

B.L.I.N.G.O. I rock the mic you rock the disco
(Tell me Bling baby what you wanna do
You're oh so fly and I'm digging you)

Hippin' it to da hop with Blingo

North of Ker-Ching up in Hipsta Hills,
The sun always shines so every Moshi chills
Hanging with my crew in da neighbourhood
You better believe it, this Fox done good

Blingo Blingo digging your lingo
Top down, seat back, paw out the window
Blingo Blingo tongue in a twist
Rockin the mic, cranking out hits

B.L.I.N.G.O. I rock the mic you rock the disco
Tell me Bling baby what you wanna do
You're oh so fly and I'm digging you)

HipHop! Binspin! Scamp! McNulty!
hats my crew but I need some more see
o grab the mic and slip on your cans
m handing on over to my Blingo fans
ingin' . . .

EY HO) F. L.A.S.H.Y.
ol, collected hip and fly
EY HO) F. L.A.S.H.Y.
aid one, two, three, clap! C'mon everybody
 the Blingo rap!

BLINGO: FAST FACTS

Profession:	**Super slick DJ, MC and funky fly rapper.**
Known for:	Rapping on other people's records.
Biggest hit to date:	**His rap on Zack Binspin's 'Moptop Tweenybop (My Hair's Too Long)'.**
Likes:	Sharp beard trimmers and chocolate coins.
Dislikes:	**Heavy Metal and anything made of silver – it's gotta be gold all the way!**
Crib:	Blingo hangs out in the Hipsta Hills overlooking Ker-Ching Canyon, but sometimes you might find him cruising along Jive Drive.
Signature move:	**The Moshi Moonwalk.**
Essential items:	Baseball cap, bling, boom box and shades!

AT HOME WITH THE STARS

Zack Binspin

When he's not hanging out with his new pal (and manager), Simon Growl, at the Sandy Drain Hotel, this particular Moptop Tweenybop likes to keep it real by getting back to his funky dustbin down in Brashcan Alley. It's here he really feels at home, surrounded by mutant sprouts, lumpy gone-off mash, and piles stinking trash.

ZACK

Dr. Strangeglove

When he's not pursuing his musical career, Dr. Strangeglove can be found lurking in any one of several secret high-tech hideouts. One of these lies deep beneath Main Street in the ancient sewerage system of Monstro City. Here, he likes nothing better than to tinker with his latest insane, criminal invention, or spend an evening turning Moshlings into Glumps with his Glumpatron 3000.

Hi Moshi music fans! When I'm not coming up with roarsome style tips, or taking in the latest fashion show showcasing this season's stellar looks, I like nothing better than hanging out at my Moshi gooperstar friend's pads, or - as Blingo calls them - their cribs! So, join me as I take you behind the scenes at home with the music stars.

Super Moshis

When they're not taking the Moshi music charts by storm, the Super Moshis are storming the strongholds of C.L.O.N.C., the enemies of all hard-working and honest Moshis everywhere. And, when they're not doing that, they like to return to their volcano base. The Super Moshi HQ is also the home of Elder Furi who watches over everything that goes on in Monstro City.

Bobbi SingSong

Already a huuuuge star back in Jollywood, Bobbi SingSong's fortune has enabled him to buy his own yoga retreat. It's here that he likes to kick back, relax and compose jolly good new tunes on his sitar.

We Heart
Poppet

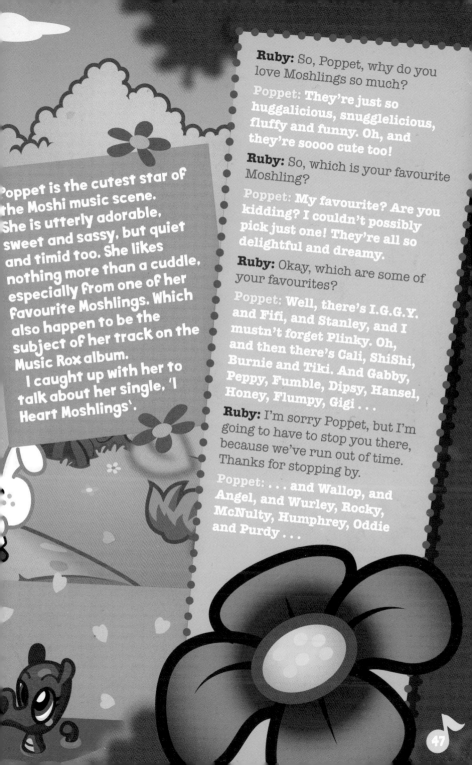

Poppet is the cutest star of the Moshi music scene. She is utterly adorable, sweet and sassy, but quiet and timid too. She likes nothing more than a cuddle, especially from one of her favourite Moshlings. Which also happen to be the subject of her track on the Music Rox album.

I caught up with her to talk about her single, 'I Heart Moshlings'.

Ruby: So, Poppet, why do you love Moshlings so much?

Poppet: They're just so huggalicious, snugglelicious, fluffy and funny. Oh, and they're soooo cute too!

Ruby: So, which is your favourite Moshling?

Poppet: My favourite? Are you kidding? I couldn't possibly pick just one! They're all so delightful and dreamy.

Ruby: Okay, which are some of your favourites?

Poppet: Well, there's I.G.G.Y. and Fifi, and Stanley, and I mustn't forget Plinky. Oh, and then there's Cali, ShiShi, Burnie and Tiki. And Gabby, Peppy, Fumble, Dipsy, Hansel, Honey, Flumpy, Gigi . . .

Ruby: I'm sorry Poppet, but I'm going to have to stop you there, because we've run out of time. Thanks for stopping by.

Poppet: . . . and Wallop, and Angel, and Wurley, Rocky, McNulty, Humphrey, Oddie and Purdy . . .

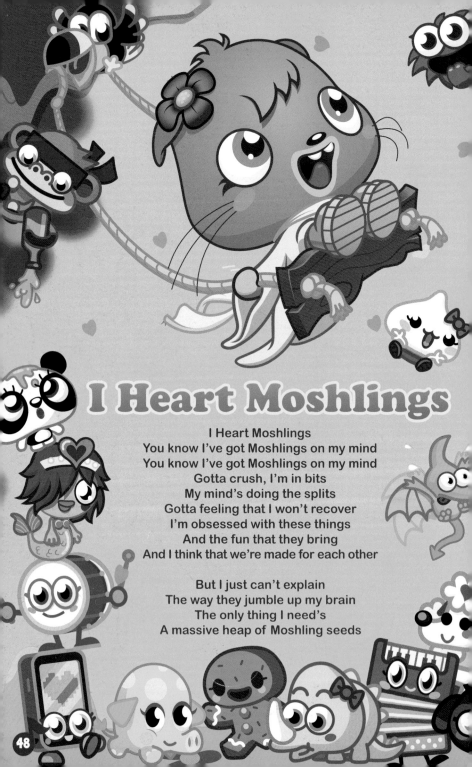

I Heart Moshlings

I Heart Moshlings
You know I've got Moshlings on my mind
You know I've got Moshlings on my mind
Gotta crush, I'm in bits
My mind's doing the splits
Gotta feeling that I won't recover
I'm obsessed with these things
And the fun that they bring
And I think that we're made for each other

But I just can't explain
The way they jumble up my brain
The only thing I need's
A massive heap of Moshling seeds

I.G.G.Y., Fifi, Stanley, Plinky, Cali, ShiShi, Burnie and Tiki
Gabby, Peppy, Fumble, Dipsy, Hansel, Honey, Flumpy and Gigi
(You know I've got Moshlings on my mind)
(You know I've got Moshlings on my mind)

They're so cute they're so cool
Got me acting the fool
I heart Moshlings, it's more than a hunch
And I think we should share
Even though mine are rare
I just gotta collect me a bunch

I.G.G.Y., Fifi, Stanley, Plinky, Cali, ShiShi, Burnie and Tiki
Gabby, Peppy, Fumble, Dipsy, Hansel, Honey, Flumpy and Gigi
Wallop, Angel, Wurley, Rocky, McNulty, Humphrey, Oddie and Purdy
Ecto, Chop Chop, Kissy, Shelby, Doris, Gurgle, oh and Mr Snoodle

But I just can't explain
The way they jumble up my brain
The only thing I need's
A massive heap of Moshling seeds

I.G.G.Y., Fifi, Stanley, Plinky, Cali, ShiShi, Burnie and Tiki
Gabby, Peppy, Fumble, Dipsy, Hansel, Honey, Flumpy and Gigi
Wallop, Angel, Wurley, Rocky, McNulty, Humphrey, Oddie and Purdy
Ecto, Chop Chop, Kissy, Shelby, Doris, Gurgle, oh and Mr Snoodle

Mr. Snoodle

Silly Snufflers are some of the sleepiest, snuffliest Moshlings around - but not Mr Snoodle. Most Silly Snufflers like to graze on the pumpernickel breadcrumbs of Franzipan Farm, while playing ice cream van melodies with their snouts - but Mr Snoodle has developed a taste for another musical style altogether. Snoodlebeat! As you can see, this Silly Snuffler is no ordinary Pony, so here are five top facts about Mr Snoodle, our very favourite Snoodlebeat Snuffler!

Mr Snoodle just can't stop doodling to the Snoodlebeat!

MR SNOODLE: FAST FACTS

1. Mr Snoodle is the meanest nose-trumpet player this side of Mount Sillimanjaro.

2. Silly Snufflers might be the sleepiest Moshlings around, but you wouldn't know it if you saw Mr Snoodle on stage. His performance certainly doesn't leave the audience yawning!

3. Mr Snoodle's favourite pastimes are snaffling pumpernickel breadcrumbs and doodling along to his CD of ice cream van melodies.

4. He loves most music, but HATES modern jazz.

5. Doodling can be done underwater and even in space!

From the Gossip Pages of Shrillboard Magazine

In my position as editor of *Shrillboard Magazine*, I see it as my duty to bring you - the Moshi music fans - all the latest gossip and tantalising titbits from the music scene. Here's the latest goss doing the rounds backstage on the Moshi Music tour.

Rumour has it that a certain famous Moshi music star is taking another so-called 'popstar' to court for mocking her signature look by wearing ridiculous costumes of her own – including one made out of chocolate-coated broccoli. More news on this as we have it.

Having recorded a rock-out cover of Zack Binspin's pop-tastic track, 'Moptop Tweenybop (My Hair's Too Long)', it is rumoured that **Zommer** is keen to work with **the Tunies** on a concept album – a rock version of Furi Feethoven's Pasteurized Symphony!

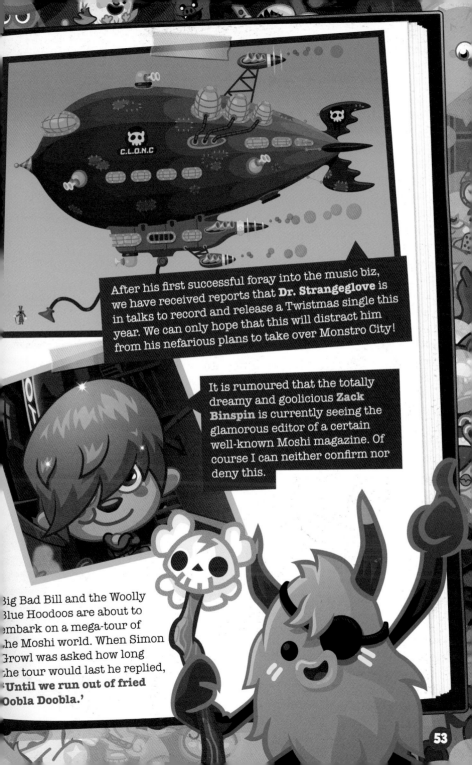

After his first successful foray into the music biz, we have received reports that **Dr. Strangeglove** is in talks to record and release a Twistmas single this year. We can only hope that this will distract him from his nefarious plans to take over Monstro City!

It is rumoured that the totally dreamy and goolicious **Zack Binspin** is currently seeing the glamorous editor of a certain well-known Moshi magazine. Of course I can neither confirm nor deny this.

Big Bad Bill and the Woolly Blue Hoodoos are about to embark on a mega-tour of the Moshi world. When Simon Growl was asked how long the tour would last he replied, '**Until we run out of fried Oobla Doobla.**'

DR. STRANGEGLOVE
& THE GLUMP GENERATION

In between Glumping innocent Moshlings, battling Elder Furi and wreaking mayhem, Dr. Strangeglove has somehow found the time to go showbiz, composing a fiendishly brilliant, semi-autobiographical song, assisted by that bumbling ball of badness, Fishlips, his trombone-playing henchGlump.

THE DOCTOR WILL SEE YOU NOW

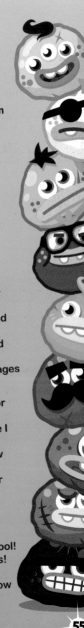

The Doctor will see you now . . . Mwahahahahahaaaa!

Sneaky, sly and shifty let me
introduce myself
I'm the doctor they call
Strangeglove,
a hazard to your health
I'm here to wreak some mayhem
with my terrifying schemes
And Glump your silly Moshlings
with my dastardly machines

[Glump chorus]
Strangeglove, Strangeglove,
they call him Dr. Strangeglove
Strangeglove, Strangeglove,
the one to be afraid of
Strangeglove, Strangeglove,
they call him Dr. Strangeglove
Strangeglove, Strangeglove,
Strangeglove, Strange

I assume you think it's sinister
to hold an ancient grudge
But understand it cost my hand
so don't be quick to judge
A Musky Husky mangled it and
chewed it like a shoe
He thought it was some sausages
so now this glove must do

Don't impede my evil deeds or
try to foil my plans
Even though I wear this glove I
have some helping hands
So peek outside your window
and check behind the door
Is Dr. Strangeglove lurking or
has he called before?

[Repeat Glump chorus]

Let 'em have it Fishlips!
Blow harder you spherical fool!
I'll show those Super Moshis!
Oh yes, nasty!
Today Monstro City, tomorrow
the world . . . the WORLD!

Ruby: Dr. Strangeglove,
it's . . . er . . . it's 'interesting'
to have you drop by and talk
about your contribution to
the Music Rox album.

Dr. Strangeglove: It's an
honour, that's what it is,
an honour!

Ruby: I'm intrigued, how did
your involvement with Simon
Growl come about?

Dr. Strangeglove: Well . . . We
had worked together before –

Ruby: When you tricked him
into unknowingly working for
your Criminal League of Naughty
Critters, you mean?

Dr. Strangeglove: Like I said,
we had worked together before,
and when that project finished
we both agreed that we could
wreak mayhem on the Moshi
music charts together when
the time was right.

Ruby: Following the success of
'The Doctor Will See You Now',
what's next for Dr. Strangeglove
and the Glump Generation?

Dr. Strangeglove: Today the
Moshi music charts, tomorrow
. . . the world! The world, I tell
you! Mwahahahahahaaaa!

55

SWEET TOOTH

Sweet Tooth is the sugary psycho who's mad, bad and dangerous to slurp. As a villainous member of C.L.O.N.C., Sweet Tooth never goes anywhere without a **Hypno Blaster lollipop**. But is this candy criminal a he or a she? That's one question I didn't ask when I met up with the candy-obsessed criminal to talk about the Gooey Glam Rock classic-in-the-making, **'Sweet Tooth Stomp.'**

Ruby: So, Sweet Tooth, does the release of 'Sweet Tooth Stomp' mark a new direction for Monstro City's most notorious dentist-hater?

Sweet Tooth: Not a chance! There's a new kinda baddie in town and I'm only just getting started.

Ruby: What was it like working with Simon Growl and HighPants Productions?

Sweet Tooth: It was totally sweet. Did you know he's got gobstopper machines all over his mansion?

Ruby: Has he really?

Sweet Tooth: Not anymore.

Ruby: So, tell us a little more about the Sweet Tooth Stomp. What made you go for the Gooey Glam Rock style?

Sweet Tooth: It's a sugar-coated, lipsmackin', candybomb, lemonade grenade of a song that will mesmerise you with its sweet sound and stick in your head like a half-chewed Scummi Bear in Zack Binspin's hair. Or is that just a side effect of my kaleidoscopic Hypno-Blaster lollipop?

Ruby: Perhaps you should quit C.L.O.N.C. and turn over a new leaf – or should that be chocolate bar? – and cut your teeth in a new career in Moshi music?

Sweet Tooth: Are you kidding me? Getting a number one record is as easy as taking candy from Baby Rox.

Sweet Tooth Stomp

Ain't life sweet!
Sweet Tooth HEY!

[Chorus]
Stomp to the beat here's a sweet candy treat
There's a new kinda baddie in town
Pink fluffy hair with a mind-blowing stare
And a face like a maniac clown

Sweet Tooth HEY!

Goody goody gumdrops
Heat seekin' lollipops
Fizz bombs 'n' treacly goo
Lemonade grenades
Lotsa sherbert cavalcades
And a gobstoppin' bubblegum chew

I'm gonna hit you with a volley
From my kaleidoscopic lolly . . .

[Repeat chorus]

Mmm, barfmallows!

Sweet Tooth HEY

Workin' for the man
Got a sugar-coated plan
And a lipsmackin' candybomb smile
Takin' over town
Gonna bring the Moshis down
With a sassafrassy sugary smile

Dealing rotten c-c-c-candy
That's my modus operandi!

[Repeat chorus]

STOP! Wonder why
You've got the urge to eat ten tons of pie?
Well maybe you been hypnotised,
kaleidobopped and mesmerised
So run away faster, escape that
swirling blaster

Ain't life sweet!

[Repeat chorus]

Goody goody gumdrops
Heat seekin' lollipops
Fizz bombs 'n' treacly goo
Lemonade grenades
Lotsa sherbert cavalcades
And a gobstoppin' bubblegum chew

[Repeat chorus]

Moshi TV
VIDEO PLAYLIST

Where can you check out the latest pop promos and virtual videos recorded by your favourite Moshi Music MonStars? Why on Moshi TV, of course

ZACK BINSPIN – MOPTOP TWEENYBOP (MY HAIR'S TOO LONG)

There's a new lid on the block and it belongs to this Tweeny-bop heart-throb who's destined for gooperstardom with his gooey ballads.

BIG BAD BILL (IS A WOOLLY BLUE HOODOO)

Buster Bumblechops is in for a surprise when he meets a tribe of Woolly Blue Hoodoos!

MR SNOODLE -
DO THE DOODLE
While the other Ponies have gone to play, Mr. Snoodle does The Doodle.

LINGO -
IGGIN YA LINGO
th DJ Quack on the cks, Blingo is rocking the sco with his crew in this arsome video.

DR. STRANGEGLOVE -
THE DOCTOR WILL SEE YOU NOW
Dr. Strangeglove hijacked Simon Growl's Highpants Recording Studio to record this song!

SUPER MOSHIS

Monstro City might look like the perfect paradise for Moshi Monsters and their Moshlings to live happily side by side, but that's only thanks to the Super Moshis. If it wasn't for these superheroes, the Criminal League of Naughty Critters would soon put a crick in everyone's day. Not content with conquering the evil masterminds and minions of C.L.O.N.C. the Super Moshis are now taking over the Moshi music pop charts!

Ruby: Hi guys! It's great of you to take time out of your busy world-saving schedule to give me all the goss on what it's like to be in the super-est super group ever.

Super Poppet: Hi Ruby. It's great to be here.

Ruby: Now tell me, how does bashing out bombastic beats compare with beating up bad guys?

Super Katsuma: It's been totally awesome! But then giving Glumps whupping is totally awesome too!

Ruby: So, what are the Super Moshis, as a band, all about?

Super Furi: We're all for truth, justice and the Moshi Monster way, Ruby. There ain't no Mount Sillimanjaro high enough, ain't no Thwack Boom Valley low enough, ain't no River Smile wide enough, to stop us from taking the

uper Moshi March to the top of
he charts.

Ruby: And what if Dr.
trangeglove or Sweet Tooth,
r someone like that, tries to spoil
hings for you?

Super Luvli: They'll soon be
aughing their evil laughs on
he other side of their faces if
hey do!

Ruby: I have to say, this latest
rack is a knock-out.

Super Zommer: It certainly
will be for Dr. Strangeglove if
he tries anything dastardly!

**Super Diavolo: Yeah! That
scheming evil genius makes
me so angry I just wanna
blow my top!**

Ruby: OK . . . Well, why don't you
let off some steam now by giving
us a rendition of your Super
Moshi March?

SUPER MOSHI MARCH

Hup, two, three, four . . .
Hup, two, three four . . .
Who do want? SUPER MOSHIS!
When do we want them? NOW

[Chorus]
Up and away
Saving the day
Hands on your hips, puff out your chest
Shout out HOORAY!
Iron your cape
Slip on your mask
Super Moshis whupped the enemy at last

Hey diddly dum dum, hey diddly dee
Now Monstro City's happy and free
Trounced Dr. Strangeglove, squished
lotsa Glumps
They deal in mischief, we deal in thumps!

Nya nana nya-na, oop doopey doo
Let's have some trumpets, blow that kazoo
Let's throw a party, start the parade
Eat tons of ice scream, glug wobble-ade

[Repeat chorus]

Tra la lala la, la la lala
Fists in the air and reach for a star
Battling baddies
Vanquishing fear
Blasting C.L.O.N.C. to the Way-Outta-Sphere!

Raise your hands as caped crusaders
Marching forth to bash invaders
Stomp your feet in celebration
You have saved the Moshi Nation!

Who do want? SUPER MOSHIS!
When do we want them? NOW
Who do want? SUPER MOSHIS!
When do we want them? NOW

[Repeat chorus]

Faster than a Wheelie YumYum!
More powerful than a Baby Blockhead!
Able to leap Sillimanjaro in a single
bound!

Is it a Birdie? Is it a SkyPony?
No, it's a SUPER MOSHI!

EXPOSED!

Caught on!

Wherever there's a Moshi music star embarrassing themselves you can guarantee that Holga the Happy Snappy won't be far away. Holga is a huge fan of Moshi music and goes to all the gigs to snap the stars as they tumble out of the Underground Disco after one too many Toad Sodas. But the Moshis know that Holga's actually their biggest fan and would never set out to make a fool of them – at least, not on purpose!

Zack Binspin and Ruby Scribblez snapped leaving the Underground Disco together

Zommer takes an accidental stage-dive!

Stashley Snoozer can't even keep his eyes open at the Underground Disco!

Bobby Singsong relaxing on Music Island

Camera

DJ Quack is rocking the ducks ··· err ··· I mean decks

Blingo pops down to Moshi TV Studios

Simon Growl ponders who is the fairest of them all?

Uh-oh, someone's had too many Wobble-ades!

Big Bad Bill storms the judging panel

MUSIC ROX!

So there you have it, Moshi music fans - all the MonStars, all the goss, in fact everything you could possibly want to know about the monsters behind the most goopendous chart-toppers of the year!

So which monster pin-up's poster is going up on your wall? Which fangtastic track is going to have you dancing round the room? Which style of music is the one that gets you in the goo-groove?

And now that you've heard all about making it in the music business, from the very best in the business, why not try starting a band with a group of your friends or jot down some lyrics for a solo effort of your own? After all, music totally Rox!

This is Ruby Scribblez signing off.
See ya later, Moshi music fans! X